MW00990968

Teach Them Spanish!

Grade K

by
Winnie Waltzer-Hackett

Carson-Dellosa Publishing LLC
Greensboro, North Carolina

04.22 – 2024

Author: Winnie Waltzer-Hackett
Editors: D'Arlyn Marks, Karen Seberg, Debra Olsen Pressnall
Spanish Consultant: Arlene Mickols
Cover Artist: Rex Schneider
Interior Artist: Janet Armbrust

Carson-Dellosa Publishing LLC
PO Box 35665
Greensboro, NC 27425 USA

ISBN 978-0-7424-0195-2
13-018217784

Table of Contents

How to Use This Book

This book presents ten units for beginning Spanish. Each unit introduces the vocabulary and includes several easy worksheet activities. Duplicate pages 6 to 47 for each child to make a booklet to store in a binder. Add activities and projects that you create. The title page of the children's booklet also serves as a sticker page. Children delight in collecting stickers at the close of each class as a reward for participation. At the end of each unit, children can color posters and take them home to display what they have learned.

The teacher's section includes lesson plans, supplemental books, sample questions for oral extension, a glossary, and an answer key. You may find it helpful to store your copy in a large ring binder with sectional dividers. The teacher lesson plans beginning on page 52 provide an outline of activities for each skill. You will find oral and physical activities to supplement the written ones.

Repetition and physical enactment are the keys to learning at this age. Not only is vocabulary repeated in each unit, but similar worksheet pages are repeated throughout the units. By completing similar activities in each unit, children will learn to work independently and gain confidence in their schoolwork. Modify the worksheets to suit your children's abilities.

It is also important to reinforce Spanish outside of the classroom. Greet children with "¡Hola!" in the hallway. Ask them to touch and name the colors of their clothing while on the playground or name some things in their lunches. These become invaluable reinforcements in learning a language. Put Spanish to use in as many school situations as possible.

Because most kindergarten children will not read, it is important to use visuals and physical action as much as possible. Save pictures from magazines to create flash cards and games. Start a collection of items to use as visual clues: a bag of used clothes, a box of colored balloons, or a collection of plastic toys. If you have a dollar store nearby, visit it frequently to look for inexpensive items. You will be surprised at how quickly your collection grows as you "think Spanish."

If you have the time, enlarge copies of the pictures from each lesson to create flash cards for the vocabulary. Children like to have a visual or physical clue when recalling vocabulary words. Focus on pronunciation and meaning of the words, not on reading and writing.

If your school desires an informal review of performance, a suggested evaluation record is included on page 71. You can observe mastery of vocabulary from Spanish to English or vice versa. It may work best to have the children tell you the Spanish word while pointing to the corresponding pictures from their booklets. Record their progress on the evaluation page.

Winnie Waltzer-Hackett

Directions for Games

Spanish Bee
A Spanish bee is a quick way to review the vocabulary in each lesson. Divide the children into teams. Use flash cards as visual aids or simply have children recall the Spanish words learned. Teams can be rewarded with points for correct answers. Alternate teams and players after each turn. No one ever sits down as in a traditional spelling bee, but each child continues to stay in the game, try again, and learn. The winning team can be rewarded with stickers or an appropriate educational token.

Bingo
This is for the teacher who is able to spend a good deal of time creating bingo cards. Your initial effort is great, and your reward will be on the children's faces as they ask to play these fun games over and over again. Enlist parents and other helpers to create the bingo cards. It is simple for the children to play with pennies as markers. Their goal is to find pictures representing four words spoken by the teacher. Bingo is a class favorite of my children, so it makes the time spent on creating bingo cards very worthwhile.

Relay Races
If you are able to make or purchase inexpensive visuals (colored beanbags, plastic food, or old clothes), you can create quick games that children will love. Have a "Spanish box" in your classroom and ask parents or children to donate items to help in learning. Relay races are fast-paced games to test quick recall of vocabulary. Call out the name of an object. Have children (divided into teams) challenge each other in finding a visual object that corresponds to the word spoken. The first team to find the correct item in the Spanish box is awarded a point.

I Spy
Play the familiar game "I spy something (verde or rojo)" to reinforce colors and other vocabulary. Have children guess the item in English (or in Spanish, if they can) until colors are mastered.

Count, Count, Count!
While not really a game, it is important to have the children count in both languages as often as possible. Seize every opportunity to count, whether it be the lunch tally, coats on the hooks, crayons in their boxes, or children wearing blue pants. The ultimate goal is to learn each Spanish number from one to ten without having to count up to ten.

IF21047 • Teach Them Spanish! K

My Spanish Book

Me llamo _____ .

 IF21047 • Teach Them Spanish! K

Introductions and Greetings

Me llamo _____ .

Let's learn some Spanish words and expressions.

¡Hola!		Hello
¿Cómo te llamas?		What is your name?
Me llamo...		My name is...
¿Cómo estás?..		How are you?

bien	mal	así, así

¡Adiós!		Good-bye

IF21047 • Teach Them Spanish! K

Pictures of Greetings

Me llamo _____ .

Listen to the words the teacher says. Circle the picture that tells the meaning of each word.

¡Hola!		
¿Cómo te llamas?		
Me llamo…		
¿Cómo estás?		
bien		
mal		
así, así		
¡Adiós!		

Greetings Paste-Up

Me llamo _____ .

 Color the picture that the teacher gives you.
Cut out each picture and glue it next to the correct word or words.

¡Hola!			¿Cómo te llamas?
Me llamo...			¿Cómo estás?
bien			mal
así, así			¡Adiós!

Numbers Introduction 1–5

Me llamo _____ .

Let's learn to count to five.

uno		1
dos	 	2
tres	  	3
cuatro	   	4
cinco	  	5

IF21047 • Teach Them Spanish! K

Numbers Review   Me llamo _____ .

 Write the number next to the Spanish word. Circle the correct number of animals for each number shown. Color the pictures.

uno [ ]

cinco [ ]

dos [ ]

cuatro [ ]

tres [ ]

Matching Numbers

Draw a line from the word to the correct picture. Color the pictures.

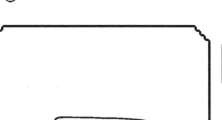

1 uno

2 dos

3 tres

4 cuatro

5 cinco

IF21047 • Teach Them Spanish! K

Number the Shoes

Me llamo _____ .

 Color and cut out the pictures that the teacher gives you.
Glue each picture next to the correct word.

uno

dos

tres

cuatro

cinco

Colors Introduction

Say the words with the teacher.
Color the word with the correct color.

IF21047 • Teach Them Spanish! K

Pictures to Color

Me llamo _____ .

 Color the pictures according to each color word.

rojo 	azul 
verde 	anaranjado 
morado 	amarillo 

Rainbow Colors

Me llamo _____ .

 Color the picture according to the color words shown.

rojo

anaranjado

amarillo

verde

azul

morado

IF21047 • Teach Them Spanish! K

Color the Cars

Me llamo _____ .

Color the cars according to the color words shown.

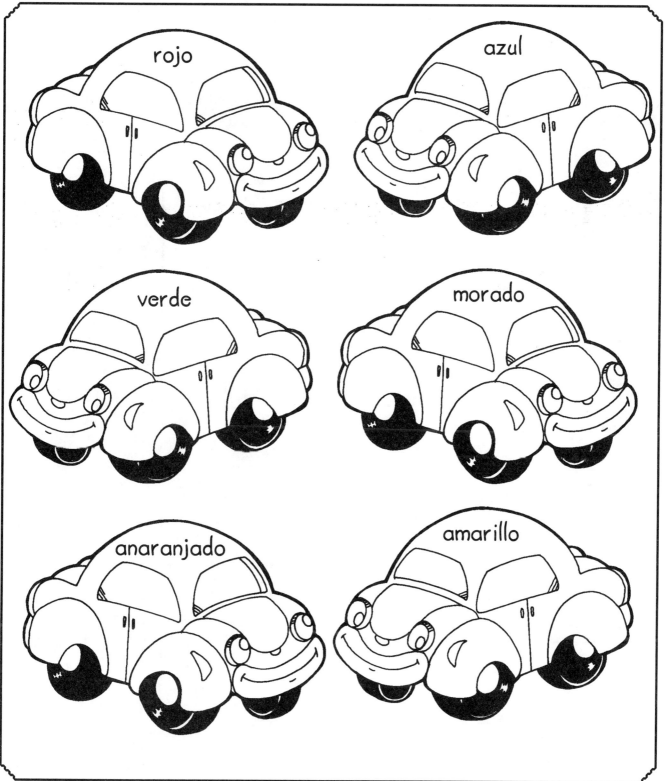

1-10 Matching

Me llamo _____ .

Tengo _____ años.

Draw a line to match each object to the number that is written in Spanish.

uno	1
dos	2
tres	3
cuatro	4
cinco	5
seis	6
siete	7
ocho	8
nueve	9
diez	10

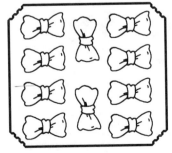

IF21047 • Teach Them Spanish! K

Count the Cookies

Me llamo _____ .

Tengo _____ años.

In each box at the left, write the number that matches the Spanish word.
X the correct number of cookies to show the number written in Spanish.
The first one is done for you.

2	dos
	cinco
	ocho
	siete
	cuatro
	diez
	uno
	nueve
	seis
	tres

Critters 1–10

Me llamo _____ .

Tengo _____ años.

 Color and cut out the pictures that the teacher gives you.
Glue each picture next to the correct number.

uno	PASTE	seis	PASTE
dos	PASTE	siete	PASTE
tres	PASTE	ocho	PASTE
cuatro	PASTE	nueve	PASTE
cinco	PASTE	diez	PASTE

20 IF21047 • Teach Them Spanish! K

My Favorite Number

Me llamo _____ .

Tengo _____ años.

Write your favorite number from 1 to 10 in the boxes.
Draw a picture to show that number.

My favorite number is [ ] .

In Spanish it is called [   ] .

Birds of Color

Me llamo _____ .

Tengo _____ años.

Color the birds according to the words listed.

azul

café

morado

rosado

rojo

verde

negro

amarillo

anaranjado

Casa de colores

Me llamo _____ .

Tengo _____ años.

 Color each crayon with the correct color for the Spanish word.
Add something with your favorite color.

café

amarillo

azul	rosado
verde	negro
amarillo	azul
blanco	rojo
rojo	amarillo
negro	café
rosado	verde

☐ rojo　☐ negro　　☐ café　☐ rosado
☐ azul　☐ amarillo　☐ blanco　☐ verde

Flores y colores

Me llamo _____ .

Tengo _____ años.

Color each flower with the correct color for the Spanish word.

☐ azul ☐ café ☐ amarillo ☐ rosado

☐ verde ☐ rojo ☐ morado ☐ anaranjado

IF21047 • Teach Them Spanish! K

 De colores

Me llamo _____ .

Tengo _____ años.

 Color and cut out the pictures that the teacher gives you.
Glue each picture next to the correct color word.

rojo	PASTE
azul	PASTE
verde	PASTE
anaranjado	PASTE
morado	PASTE

amarillo	PASTE
café	PASTE
negro	PASTE
blanco	PASTE
rosado	PASTE

25

Classroom Things

Me llamo _____ .

Tengo _____ años.

Let's learn some Spanish classroom words.

| silla |  | chair |

| libro | | book |

| mesa |  | table |

| lápiz | | pencil |

| tijeras |  | scissors |

| borrador | | eraser |

Matching Objects

Me llamo _____ .

Tengo _____ años.

Draw a line from the word to the correct picture. Color the picture.

silla

libro

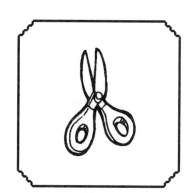

mesa

lápiz

tijeras

borrador

IF21047 • Teach Them Spanish! K

Draw and Color Your Classroom

Me llamo _____ .

Tengo _____ años.

Draw and color a picture for each word listed.
Which ones do you have in your classroom? Circle them.

silla

libro

mesa

lápiz

tijeras

borrador

Match Pictures and Words

Me llamo _____ .

Tengo _____ años.

Color the pictures on the page that the teacher gives you.
Cut out the pictures and glue each picture next to the correct word.

silla	
borrador	
mesa	

 lápiz

 tijeras

 libro

IF21047 • Teach Them Spanish! K

Family Words

Me llamo _____ .

Tengo _____ años.

Let's learn some Spanish family words.

madre		mother
padre		father
chica		girl
chico		boy
abuela		grandma
abuelo		grandpa

IF21047 • Teach Them Spanish! K

Draw Your Family

Me llamo _____ .

Tengo _____ años.

Draw a picture of your family. Color your picture.

Mi familia

Do you remember the words listed below? If you can, write the correct Spanish word next to each person in your picture above.

padre	chico	abuelo
madre	chica	abuela

Family Word Meanings

Me llamo _____ .

Tengo _____ años.

Listen to the words that the teacher says.
Circle the picture that shows the meaning of each word.

padre		
chica		
abuela		
madre		
abuelo		
chico		

     IF21047 • Teach Them Spanish! K

Matching Family

Me llamo _____ .

Tengo _____ años.

Color and cut out the pictures that the teacher gives you.
Glue each picture next to the correct word.

padre		chica	
madre		abuelo	
chico		abuela	

Try this:

Color each block with a letter inside. Do not color the blocks with numbers.
What hidden word did you find? Do you know what it means?

2	2	2	2	2	2	2	2	2	2	2	2	m	2	2	2	2	2	2	2	2
2	2	2	2	2	2	2	2	2	2	2	2	m	2	2	2	2	2	2	2	2
m	m	m	m	m	2	m	m	m	2	2	m	m	m	2	m	m	m	2	m	m	m
m	2	m	2	m	2	m	2	m	2	2	m	2	m	2	m	2	m	2	m	2
m	2	m	2	m	2	m	2	m	2	2	m	2	m	2	m	2	2	2	m	m	m
m	2	m	2	m	2	m	2	m	2	2	m	2	m	2	m	2	2	m	m	m
m	2	m	2	m	2	m	2	m	2	2	m	2	m	2	m	2	2	2	m	2	2
m	2	m	2	m	2	m	m	m	m	2	m	m	m	2	m	2	2	2	m	m	m

IF21047 • Teach Them Spanish! K

Food and Drink

Me llamo _____ .

Tengo _____ años.

Let's learn the Spanish words for food and drinks.

queso		cheese
leche		milk
papa		potato
jugo		juice
pan	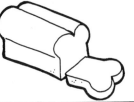	bread
pollo		chicken
ensalada		salad

© Carson-Dellosa

IF21047 • Teach Them Spanish! K

 **My Meal**

Food

Me llamo _____ .

Tengo _____ años.

 Color, cut out, then glue on the pictures that the teacher gives you to make a meal. Which food is your favorite?

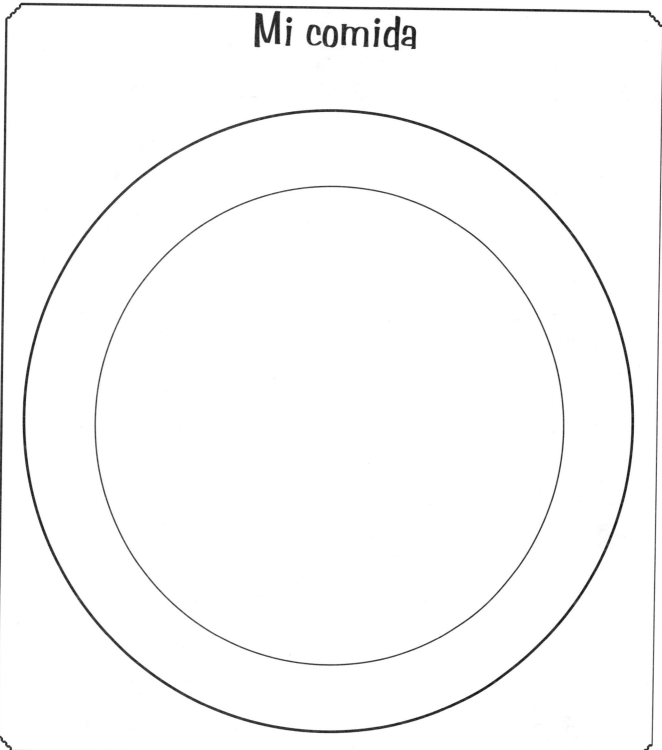

Mi comida

© Carson-Dellosa

35

IF21047 • Teach Them Spanish! K

Food Meanings

Me llamo _____ .

Tengo _____ años.

 Listen to the words that the teacher says. Circle the picture that shows the meaning of each word.

papa		
ensalada		
queso		
pan		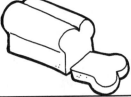
leche		
pollo		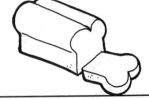
jugo		

IF21047 • Teach Them Spanish! K

Mixed-Up Food

Me llamo _____ .

Tengo _____ años.

Draw a line from the word to the food picture.

papa

ensalada

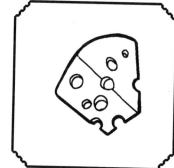

queso

pan

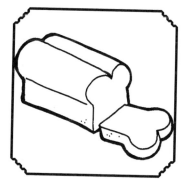

leche

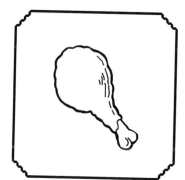

jugo

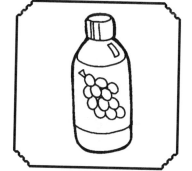

pollo

© Carson-Dellosa

37

IF21047 • Teach Them Spanish! K

Clothing

Me llamo _____ .

Tengo _____ años.

Let's learn some Spanish clothing words.

camisa		shirt
pantalones		pants
vestido		dress
calcetines		socks
zapatos		shoes
gorro		cap

IF21047 • Teach Them Spanish! K

Clothing Match-Ups

Me llamo _____ .

Tengo _____ años.

Draw a line from the word to match the correct picture. Color the picture.

camisa

pantalones

zapatos

gorro

vestido

calcetines

How Are You?

Me llamo _____ .

Tengo _____ años.

Use the pictures that your teacher gives you to make a boy or girl. Color, cut out, and glue on the face and clothes that you like. Draw your own hair.

IF21047 • Teach Them Spanish! K

Clothes to Color

Me llamo _____ .

Tengo _____ años.

Color and cut out the pictures that the teacher gives you.
Glue each picture next to the correct word.

| camisa |  | zapatos |  |

| calcetines | | vestido | |

| pantalones | | gorro |  |

Try this:

Color each block with a letter X inside. Do not color the blocks with numbers. What hidden word did you find? Do you know what it means?

8	8	8	8	8	8	8	8	8	8	8	8	8	8	8	8	8	8	8	8	8	8
8	8	x	x	x	8	x	x	x	8	x	x	x	8	x	x	x	8	x	x	x	8
8	8	x	8	x	8	x	8	x	8	x	8	x	8	x	8	x	8	x	8	x	8
8	8	x	x	x	8	x	8	x	8	x	8	8	8	x	8	8	8	x	8	x	8
8	8	8	8	x	8	x	x	x	8	x	8	8	8	x	8	8	8	x	x	x	8
8	8	x	8	x	8	8	8	8	8	x	8	8	8	x	8	8	8	8	8	8	8
8	8	x	x	x	8	8	8	8	8	8	8	8	8	8	8	8	8	8	8	8	8

Places to Go

Me llamo _____ .

Tengo _____ años.

Where do you like to go? Let's learn some Spanish words
for places in our community.

| escuela |  | school |

| museo |  | museum |

| casa |  | house |

| tienda |  | store |

| biblioteca |  | library |

| parque | | park |

IF21047 • Teach Them Spanish! K

Picture This!

Me llamo _____ .

Tengo _____ años.

Listen to the words the teacher says.
Circle the picture that shows the meaning of each word.

casa		

escuela		

tienda		

parque		

biblioteca		

museo		

My Neighborhood

Me llamo _____ .

Tengo _____ años.

Draw a picture of an imaginary neighborhood.
Draw places you have learned about in this unit. Add streets, trees, and whatever else you wish to make your neighborhood look nice. Color your picture.

Mi barrio

Can you label your neighborhood with the words we learned?

casa   parque   biblioteca   tienda   escuela   museo

Places, Please

Me llamo _____ .

Tengo _____ años.

 Color and cut out the pictures that the teacher gives you.
Glue each picture next to the correct word.

casa		tienda	
parque		escuela	
biblioteca		museo	

Try this:
Color each block with a letter Y inside. Do not color the blocks with numbers.
What hidden word did you find? Do you know what it means?

9	9	9	9	9	9	9	9	9	9	9	9	9	9	9	9
y	y	y	9	y	y	y	9	9	y	y	y	9	y	y	9
y	9	y	9	y	9	y	9	9	y	9	9	9	y	9	9
y	9	9	9	y	9	y	9	9	y	y	y	9	y	9	9
y	9	y	9	y	9	y	9	9	9	9	y	9	y	9	9
y	y	y	9	y	y	y	y	9	y	y	y	9	y	y	y
9	9	9	9	9	9	9	9	9	9	9	9	9	9	9	9

Dot-to-Dot

Me llamo _____ .

Tengo _____ años.

Connect the dots. Start with the Spanish word one (uno). Draw a line to two (dos). Continue up to ten (diez). What shape did you get?

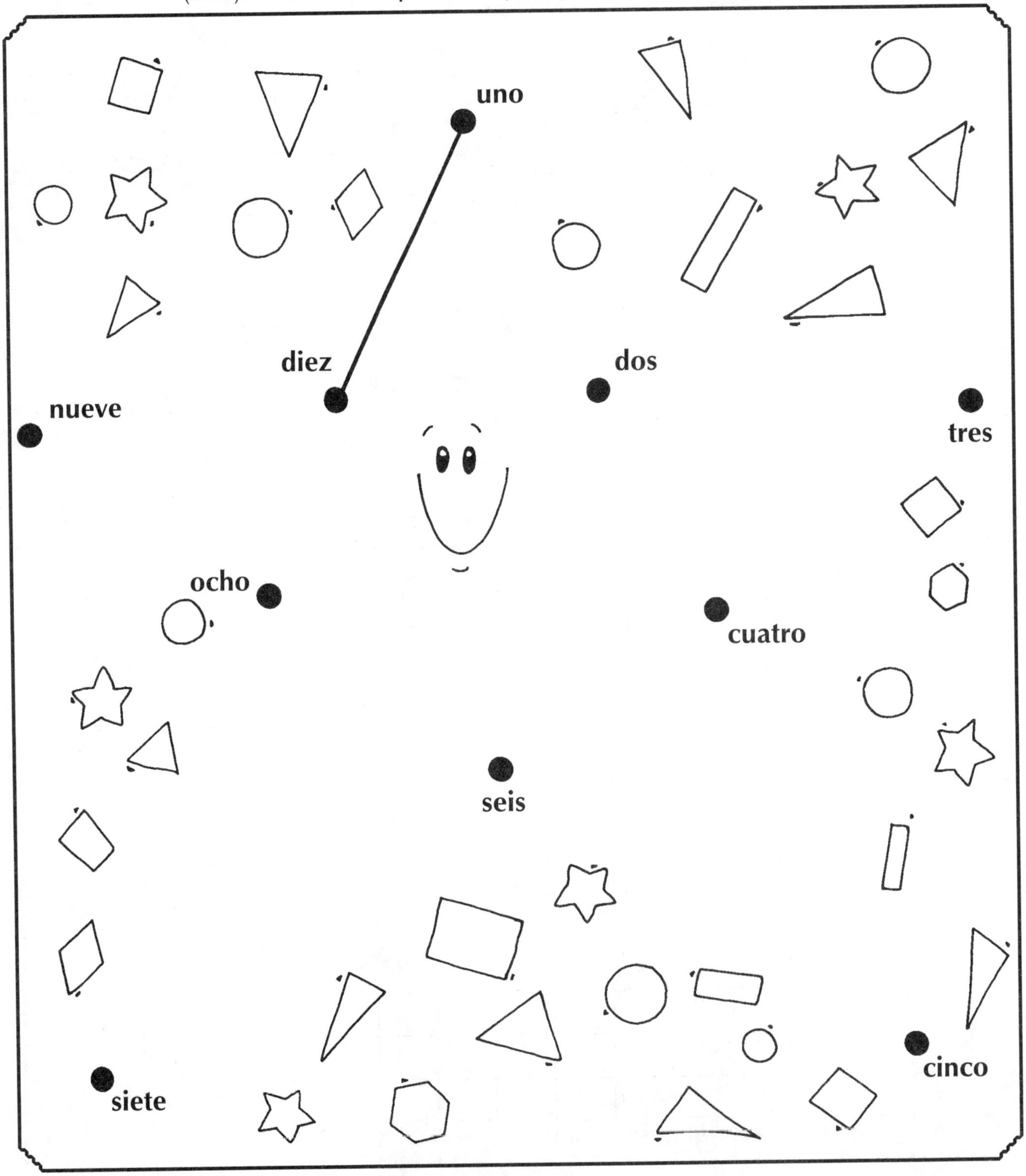

uno

diez

dos

nueve

tres

ocho

cuatro

seis

siete

cinco

IF21047 • Teach Them Spanish! K

Great Start in Spanish!

Awarded to _____

on _____

by _____

IF21047 • Teach Them Spanish! K

Songs and Chants

The Pledge of Allegiance

Juro fidelidad a la bandera
de los Estados Unidos de América,
y a la república que representa,
una nación bajo Dios indivisible
con libertad y justicia para todos.

¡Hola! Means Hello
(to the tune of "London Bridge")

¡Hola! means hello-o-o, hello-o-o, hello-o-o.
¡Hola! means hello-o-o. ¡Hola, amigos!

¡Adiós! Means Good-bye
(to the tune of "London Bridge")

¡Adiós! means goo-ood-bye, goo-ood-bye, goo-ood-bye.
¡Adiós! means goo-ood-bye. ¡Adiós, amigos!

¡Adios!

Cinco amigos
(to the tune of "Ten Little Fingers")

Uno, dos, tres, cuatro, cinco,
Uno, dos, tres, cuatro, cinco,
Uno, dos, tres, cuatro, cinco,
Cinco amigos son.

IF21047 • Teach Them Spanish! K

Songs and Chants

Diez amigos
(to the tune of "Ten Little Fingers")

Uno, dos, tres amigos,
cuatro, cinco, seis amigos,
siete, ocho, nueve amigos,
diez amigos son.

Diez, nueve, ocho amigos,
siete, seis, cinco amigos,
cuatro, tres, dos amigos,
un amigo es.

Colors Song
(to the tune of "Twinke, Twinkle Little Star")

Red is rojo,   green is verde,
purple, morado,   brown, café;
yellow, amarillo,   blue, azul,
pink is rosado,   orange, anaranjado;
white is blanco,   black is negro,
colors, colores,   colors, colores.

Classroom Objects Song
(to the tune of "The Farmer in the Dell")

A silla is a chair;
A libro is a book;
A mesa is a table in our classroom.

A lápiz is a pencil;
Tijeras is a scissors;
A borrador is an eraser in our classroom.

Songs and Chants

Family Song
(to the tune of "Are You Sleeping?")

Padre — father
madre — mother
chico — boy
chica — girl
abuelo is a grandpa
abuela is a grandma
nuestra familia, our family.

Clothing Song
(to the tune of "Skip to My Lou")

Camisa — shirt,   pantalones — pants,
vestido — dress,   calcetines — socks,
zapatos — shoes,   gorro — cap
These are the clothes that we wear.

Cumpleaños feliz
(to the tune of "Happy Birthday")

Cumpleaños feliz,
cumpleaños feliz,
Te deseamos todos,
cumpleaños feliz.

Songs and Chants

Food Song
(to the tune of "She'll Be Coming 'Round the Mountain")

Queso is cheese, yum, yum, yum. (clap, clap)
Leche is milk, yum, yum, yum. (clap, clap)
Papa is potato.
Jugo is juice.
Pan is bread, yum, yum, yum! (clap, clap)

Pollo is chicken, yum, yum, yum. (clap, clap)
Ensalada is salad, yum, yum, yum. (clap, clap)
Queso, leche, papa,
jugo, pan, pollo, ensalada,
yum, yum, yum, yum, yum! (clap, clap)

Noche de paz
("Silent Night")

Noche de paz, noche de amor,
todo duerme en derredor.
Entre los astros que esparcen la luz,
bella anunciando al niño Jesús.
Brilla la estrella de paz,
Brilla la estrella de paz.

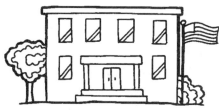

Community Song
(to the tune of "Here We Go 'Round the Mulberry Bush")

Escuela is school,   museo museum;
casa is house,   tienda is store;
biblioteca is library;   parque is the park for me!

Lesson Plans

Introduction to Spanish
Kindergarten

This book is written as an introduction to basic Spanish. Worksheets are available for each lesson. Do not hesitate to introduce written Spanish to children this young. Whether they are able to read or not, the exposure to the written words along with the pictures create a nice balance for children of all ability levels. Let those who wish to learn the written words do so. Let others learn through the sounds of the words and the accompanying pictures. Experience has shown me that young students are very enthusiastic about learning a new language.

Take your time! Some children may catch on more quickly than others. Repetition is the key word. Review each set of lessons as much as needed before moving on to the next topic. Make overhead transparencies of unit intro pages. Students can point to the words as you say them aloud as a class. I suggest about a 30-minute class period for each worksheet and activities. Feel free to expand on the given lesson plans. Be creative and add to the list of activities.

The shapes on the cover of the child's "My Spanish Book" title page are to be used for reward stickers. I recommend giving each student a reward sticker at the end of each class for participating and completing the daily activities. Make additional sticker pages if students fill up their cover pages.

The two books listed below are great to use on your first day of class. Children will love the illustrations and may realize that they already know many Spanish words. Enjoy!

Page	Activity	Directions	Materials
6-47	Preparation and distribution of books	Photocopy student books. Have students store them in ring binders.	photocopies of student pages one ring binder per student
6	Title page		small stickers to use as rewards
	Book — oral reading	Read Say Hola to Spanish to introduce students to the concept of another language. Discuss Spanish words used in the book that they may already know.	Say Hola to Spanish by Susan Middleton Elya
	Book — oral reading	Read Say Hola to Spanish, Otra Vez to review the concept of another language. Discuss Spanish words used in the book that they may already know.	Say Hola to Spanish, Otra Vez by Susan Middleton Elya

Lesson Plans

Introductions and Greetings

¡Hola! — Hello!
¿Cómo te llamas? — What's your name?
Me llamo... — My name is...
¡Adiós! — Good-bye!

Kindergarten

¿Cómo estás? — How are you?
bien — fine
mal — bad(ly)
así, así — so-so

Page	Activity	Directions	Materials
7	worksheet—Introductions and Greetings	Look at pictures. Repeat words then color the pictures.	colored pencils or crayons
48	song—"Hola Means Hello"	Learn and sing an appropriate song to begin each class.	Song and Chants page 48
	roll call	Each class have students answer roll call with ¡Hola!.	
	What's your name?	Each class have students practice answering the question ¿Cómo te llamas? until they are familiar with the question and response.	
	How are you?	Each class ask students how they are. They should respond with the words and proper hand signal: bien — thumbs up, mal — thumbs down, así, así — flat hand rotating.	
8	worksheet—Pictures of Greetings	Review words and meanings. Circle the corresponding picture.	pencils
9 + Teacher Aids	worksheet—Greetings Paste-Up	Have children color the pictures, cut out each box, and paste it next to the corresponding word/s on page 9.	Teacher Aids page 63, colored pencils or crayons, scissors, glue stick
	greetings poster	Color a greetings poster.	photocopies (pages 79–80) assembled to create an 11 x 17 inch (28 x 43 cm) page, crayons
	class departure	Each class have students leave while saying ¡Adiós!.	
48	song—"¡Adiós! Means Good-bye"	Learn and sing an appropriate song to end each class.	Song and Chants page 48

IF21047 • Teach Them Spanish! K

Lesson Plans

Numbers 1–5   Kindergarten

uno – one	cuatro – four
dos – two	cinco – five
tres – three	

Page	Activity	Directions	Materials
10	worksheet—Numbers Introduction 1–5	Repeat numbers and count the items for each number. Color pictures.	colored pencils or crayons
48	song –"Cinco amigos"	Learn and sing a counting song each class.	Songs and Chants page 48, use page 10 as a visual
	classroom counting	Practice counting things in the classroom (up to 5) each class.	
11	worksheet—Numbers Review	Children write the number for each word. Circle the correct number of pictures for each number. Color the pictures.	colored pencils or crayons
	roll 'em	Have students roll a large foam die and count the dots.	large foam die
	beanbag counting	Count beanbags while tossing them into a basket.	5 colored beanbags, basket or plastic tub
12	worksheet— Matching Numbers	Draw a line from the word to the correct picture. Color the pictures.	colored pencils or crayons
	numbers bingo	Find the number that corresponds to the word spoken by the teacher. See page 75 for details.	pages 76 and 78, bingo cards, pennies or markers
13 + Teacher Aids	worksheet—Number the Shoes	Color each picture. Cut out and paste each picture next to the corresponding number.	Teacher Aids page 63, colored pencils or crayons, scissors, glue stick
	dominoes	Have students count the number of dots on dominoes (up to five).	dominoes (regular or make your own)

**Continue to practice numbers 1-5 for mastery while the next unit is introduced.
Numbers 6-10 will be introduced after the colors unit.**

Lesson Plans

Colors (Part 1)   Kindergarten

rojo — red   amarillo — yellow
azul — blue   morado — purple
verde — green   anaranjado — orange

Page	Activity	Directions	Materials
14	worksheet—Colors Introduction	Have the children repeat words and learn their meanings. Color the words according to their meanings.	colored pencils or crayons
	find classroom colors	Have the children find items in the classroom that are the color that the teacher names.	classroom items
	find the crayons	Students select the six crayon colors (listed above) that are taught in this unit. Students practice saying the names in Spanish as they hold up the corresponding crayons.	box of crayons per student
15	worksheet—Pictures to Color	Color the pictures for each word.	colored pencils or crayons
	Who's wearing...?	Ask students to examine their clothing. Raise hands when they find they are wearing clothing of the color named.	
16	worksheet—Rainbow Colors	Color the picture according to the words written in Spanish.	colored pencils or crayons
	beanbag search	Students take turns finding the beanbag requested, using the Spanish color word.	basket of colored beanbags
	I Spy	Students play I Spy (for example, "I spy somthing verde") using Spanish color words. Other students try to guess the object.	
17	worksheet—Color the Cars	Students color the cars according to the words written in Spanish.	colored pencils or crayons
	colors bingo	Children find the color that corresponds to the word that the teacher says. See page 75 for details.	pages 76 and 78, bingo cards, pennies or markers

**Continue to practice color words for mastery while the next unit is introduced.
Four more colors will be introduced after the next unit.**

Lesson Plans

Numbers 1–10 (review and extension)   Kindergarten

uno — one   cinco — five   ocho — eight
dos — two   seis — six   nueve — nine
tres — three   siete — seven   diez — ten
cuatro — four

Page	Activity	Directions	Materials
18	worksheet—1–10 Matching	Repeat numbers; count and match the objects. (Note: Students now begin to write their ages at the top of the page. Encourage them to write the number word in Spanish, not the numeral.)	colored pencils or crayons
49	song —"Diez amigos"	Learn and sing a counting song each class.	Songs and Chants page 49
	classroom counting	Each class counts the number of boys and girls.	
19	worksheet—Count the Cookies	Repeat numbers; cross off the correct number of cookies to show each number listed.	colored pencils or crayons
	beanbag counting	Count beanbags while tossing them into a basket.	10 colored beanbags, basket or plastic tub
20 + Teacher Aids	worksheet—Critters 1–10	Color each picture (optional). Cut out each picture and paste it to the square next to the corresponding number.	Teacher Aids page 64, colored pencils, scissors, glue stick
21	worksheet—My Favorite Number	Write your favorite number and the Spanish word for it. Then draw and color that number of objects.	pencil colored pencils or crayons
	roll 'em	Children roll a large foam die and count the dots.	large foam die
Teacher Aids	numbers paper chain	Color or decorate strips then cut them apart before gluing into a paper chain.	photocopies of page 69 on construction paper, glue sticks, scissors, colored pencils or crayons
	numbers bingo	Find the number that corresponds to the word spoken by the teacher. See page 75 for details.	pages 77 and 78, bingo cards, pennies or markers
	numbers poster	Color a numbers poster.	photocopies (pages 81–82) assembled to create an 11 x 17 inch (28 x 43 cm) page, crayons

Continue to practice numbers for mastery throughout the year.

Lesson Plans

Colors (Part 2)   Kindergarten

rojo — red	morado — purple	blanco — white
azul — blue	café — brown	amarillo — yellow
verde — green	negro — black	rosado — pink
anaranjado — orange		

Page	Activity	Directions	Materials
22	worksheet—Birds of Color	Fill in a color key on the board, together as a class. Color the birds according to the Spanish color words.	colored pencils or crayons
49	"Colors Song"	Learn and sing a colors song each class.	Songs and Chants page 49
23	worksheet—Casa de colores	Fill in the color key at the bottom together as a class. Color each crayon according to the word listed.	colored pencils or crayons
	Find it!	Find items in the classroom that are the color named by the teacher.	clothing/classroom items
24	worksheet—Flores y colores	Fill in the color key at the bottom together as a class. Color each flower according to the word listed.	colored pencils or crayons
	beanbag relay (team challenge)	Students race to baskets and find the color that the teacher names in Spanish.	20 beanbags — two of each color
25 + Teacher Aids	worksheet—De colores	Color each picture. Cut out and paste each picture onto the square next to the corresponding word.	Teacher Aids page 64, colored pencils, scissors, glue stick
Teacher Aids	colors paper chain	Color strips accordingly, cut, and assemble into a paper chain.	photocopies of page 70 on construction paper, glue sticks, scissors, crayons
	I Spy	Students play I Spy using Spanish color words.	
	colors bingo	Find the color that corresponds to the word spoken by the teacher. See page 75 for details.	pages 77 and 78, bingo cards, pennies or markers
	colors poster	Color a poster of color words and things.	photocopies (pages 83–84) assembled to create an 11 x 17 inch (28 x 43 cm) page, crayons

Continue to practice color words for mastery throughout the year.

Lesson Plans

Classroom Objects

Kindergarten

silla — chair
mesa — table
tijeras — scissors

libro — book
lápiz — pencil
borrador — eraser

Page	Activity	Directions	Materials
26	worksheet—Classroom Things	Repeat classroom words then color the illustrations.	colored pencils or crayons
49	"Classroom Objects Song"	Learn and sing a classroom objects song.	Song and Chants page 49, use page 26 as a visual
27	worksheet—Matching Objects	Draw a line from the word to the correctr picture. Color the pictures.	colored pencils or crayons
Teacher Aids	label the classroom	Children cut out classroom words then find the object and tape the word to it.	Teacher Aids page 66, scissors, tape
28	worksheet—Draw and Color Your Classroom	Draw and color classroom objects, then circle those found in your classroom.	colored pencils or crayons
	Guess what?	Teacher thinks of an object. Give students clues using Spanish color words. Have the students guess using the Spanish words.	classroom objects
29 + Teacher Aids	worksheet—Match Pictures and Words	Color and cut out each picture and paste it to the square next to the corresponding word.	Teacher Aids page 65, colored pencils or, scissors, glue sticks
	scavenger hunt (team challenge)	Students have one minute to locate the three objects assigned by the teacher. Points are given to the team if they meet the challenge.	index cards with random groups of three objects (words written in Spanish, read to the team by the teacher)
	classroom objects bingo	Find the picture that corresponds to the word that the teacher says. See page 75 for details.	pages 76 and 78, bingo cards, pennies or markers
	classroom objects poster	Color a classroom objects poster.	photocopies (pages 85–86) assembled to create an 11 x 17 inch (28 x 43 cm) page, crayons

IF21047 • Teach Them Spanish! K

Lesson Plans

Family   Kindergarten

padre – father	madre – mother
chico – boy	chica – girl
abuelo – grandpa	abuela – grandma

Page	Activity	Directions	Materials
30	worksheet—Family Words (introduction)	Repeat family words then color the illustrations.	colored pencils or crayons
50	"Family Song"	Learn and sing a family song.	Song and Chants page 50, use page 30 as a visual
31	worksheet—Draw Your Family	Draw and color a picture of your own family. Label with the Spanish words if you can.	colored pencils or crayons
	counting practice	Have students answer: ¿Cuántos chicos hay? (How many boys are there?) ¿Cuántas chicas hay? (How many girls are there?) by counting boys and girls in the classroom.	
32	worksheet—Family Word Meanings	Review words and meanings. Circle the corresponding picture. Color the pictures.	pencils, colored pencils
	Guess who?	Think of a family member. Give students clues. Have the students guess who, using the Spanish word.	
33 + Teacher Aids	worksheet—Matching Family	Color each picture. Cut out and paste each picture on the square next to the corresponding word.	Teacher Aids page 65, colored pencils or crayons, scissors, glue stick
	family bingo	Find the picture that corresponds to the word that the teacher says. See page 75 for details.	pages 76 and 78, bingo cards, pennies or markers
	family poster	Color a family poster.	photocopies (pages 87–88) assembled to create an 11 x 17 inch (28 x 43 cm) page, crayons

Lesson Plans

Food   Kindergarten

queso – cheese	pan – bread
leche – milk	pollo – chicken
papa – potato	ensalada – salad
jugo – juice	

Page	Activity	Directions	Materials
34	worksheet—Food and Drink	Repeat food words then color the illustrations.	colored pencils or crayons
51	"Food Song"	Learn and sing a food song.	Songs and Chants page 51, use page 34 as a visual
35 + Teacher Aids	worksheet—My Meal	Color, cut out food pictures, and glue them to the page to create a meal.	Teacher Aids page 66, colored pencils or crayons, scissors, glue sticks
	food practice – ¿Qué es?	Children take turns naming the food that the teacher shows, using the Spanish words.	plastic food from toy store or real food/food containers from home
36	worksheet—Food Meanings	Review words and meanings. Circle each corresponding picture. Color the pictures.	pencils, colored pencils
	Guess what?	Think of a food/drink. Give students clues. Have the students use the Spanish word to guess what it is.	
37 +	worksheet—Mixed-Up Food	Draw a line from the word to the food picture.	
	food bingo	Find the picture that corresponds to the word spoken by the teacher. See page 75 for details.	pages 77 and 78, bingo cards, pennies or markers
	food poster	Color a food poster.	photocopies (pages 89–90) assembled to create an 11 x 17 inch (28 x 43 cm) page, crayons

     IF21047 • Teach Them Spanish! K

Lesson Plans

Clothing   Kindergarten

camisa — shirt   calcetines — socks
pantalones — pants   zapatos — shoes
vestido — dress   gorro — cap

Page	Activity	Directions	Materials
38	worksheet—Clothing	Repeat clothing words then color the illustrations.	colored pencils or crayons
50	"Clothing Song"	Sing a song using clothing vocabulary.	Songs and Chants page 50, use page 38 as a visual
39	worksheet—Clothing Match-Ups	Draw a line from the word to the correct pictures.	colored pencils or crayons
	Who's wearing...? What color is it?	Ask students who is wearing clothing (using Spanish words learned) and have them tell the color in Spanish (using words learned).	
40 + Teacher Aids	worksheet—How Are You?	Color clothing and faces from the accompanying pages. Then, listen to the teacher ask for clothing, faces (bien, mal, así, así), or gender. Use the appropriate pictures to create your likeness. Draw the hair.	colored pencils or crayons, Teacher Aids page 67, scissors, envelopes to store pictures
	find the clothing (team relay/challenge)	Children find the item of clothing that the teacher names in Spanish.	basket of clothing, two of each item of clothing
41 + Teacher Aids	worksheet—Clothes to Color	Color and cut out each picture and paste it on the square next to the corresponding word.	Teacher Aids page 68, colored pencils or crayons, scissors, glue stick
	clothing bingo	Find the picture that corresponds to the word spoken by the teacher. See page 75 for details.	pages 76 and 78, bingo cards, pennies or markers
	clothing poster	Color a clothing poster.	photocopies (pages 91–92) assembled to create an 11 x 17 inch (28 x 43 cm) page, crayons

IF21047 • Teach Them Spanish! K

Lesson Plans

Community

Kindergarten

escuela — school
museo — museum
casa — house

tienda — store
biblioteca — library
parque — park

Page	Activity	Directions	Materials
42	worksheet—Places to Go	Repeat community words then color the illustrations.	colored pencils or crayons
51	"Community Song"	Sing a song using community vocabulary.	Songs and Chants page 51, use page 42 as a visual
43	worksheet—Picture This!	Review words and meanings. Circle the corresponding picture. Color the pictures.	colored pencils or crayons
	book scavenger hunt (team challenge)	Use picture books in the classroom to find images of community words.	picture books
44	worksheet—My Neighborhood	Create a picture of an imaginary neighborhood using the place words. Children label the picture if possible.	colored pencils or crayons
	Guess what?	Think of a place or building in the community. Give students clues. Have the students guess what place by using the Spanish word.	
45 + Teacher Aids	worksheet—Places, Please	Color each picture. Cut out each picture and paste it on the square next to the corresponding word.	Teacher Aids page 68, colored pencils or crayons, scissors, glue stick
	community bingo	Find the picture that corresponds to the word spoken by the teacher. See page 75 for details.	pages 76 and 78, bingo cards, pennies or markers
	community poster	Color a community poster.	photocopies (pages 93–94) assembled to create an 11 x 17 inch (28 x 43 cm) page, crayons

Numbers Review & Year-End Award

Page 46 may serve as an evaluative tool before departing for the summer.

46	worksheet—Dot-to-Dot	Connect the dots in order from uno to diez.	pencils, crayons
47	year-end award	Give each child a personalized "Great Start in Spanish!" award certificate.	photocpies, sign an award for each child

Teacher Aids

Pictures for use with page 9

Pictures for use with page 13

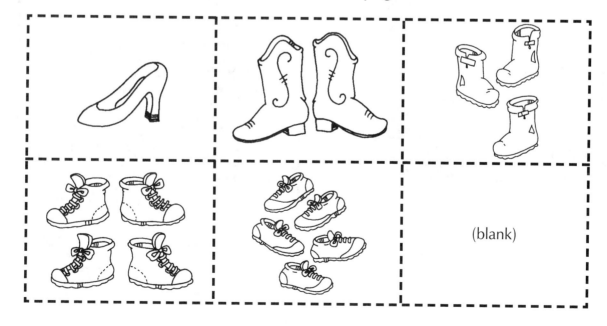

(blank)

63   IF21047 • Teach Them Spanish! K

Teacher Aids

Pictures for use with page 20   Pictures for use with page 25

          IF21047 • Teach Them Spanish! K

Teacher Aids

Pictures for use with page 29

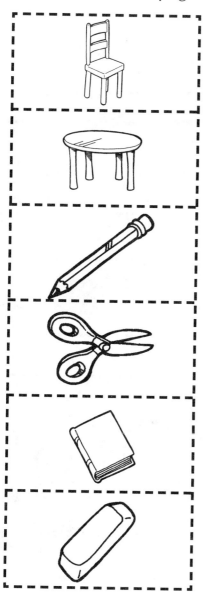

Pictures for use with page 33

Teacher Aids

Label the classroom

silla	mesa
borrador	tijeras
libro	lápiz

Pictures for use with My Meal (page 35)

IF21047 • Teach Them Spanish! K

Teacher Aids

Pictures for use on page 40

IF21047 • Teach Them Spanish! K

Teacher Aids

Pictures for use with page 41

Pictures for use with page 45

IF21047 • Teach Them Spanish! K

Teacher Aids

Numbers paper chain

	uno	
	dos	
	tres	
	cuatro	
	cinco	
	seis	
	siete	
	ocho	
	nueve	
	diez	

Teacher Aids

Colors paper chain

🍓	**rojo**	🍓
🐦	**azul**	🐦
🍐	**verde**	🍐
○	**anaranjado**	○
🍇	**morado**	🍇
☀	**amarillo**	☀
▭	**café**	▭
🦇	**negro**	🦇
❄	**blanco**	❄
🐷	**rosado**	🐷

IF21047 • Teach Them Spanish! K

Student Evaluation Record

Name _____

School Year _____

Introductions and Greetings   Date tested _____

- ☐ ¡Hola! — Hello
- ☐ ¿Cómo te llamas? — What's your name?
- ☐ bien — fine
- ☐ así, así — so-so
- ☐ Me llamo — My name is...
- ☐ ¿Cómo estás? — How are you?
- ☐ mal _ bad
- ☐ ¡Adiós! — Goodbye

☐ **Percentage mastered**

Numbers 1–5   Date tested _____

1   2   3   4   5
☐   ☐   ☐   ☐   ☐

☐ **Percentage mastered**

Colors (Part 1)   Date tested _____

- ☐ rojo — red
- ☐ verde — green
- ☐ morado — purple
- ☐ azul — blue
- ☐ amarillo — yellow
- ☐ anaranjado — orange

☐ **Percentage mastered**

Numbers 1–10   Date tested _____

1   2   3   4   5   6   7   8   9   10
☐   ☐   ☐   ☐   ☐   ☐   ☐   ☐   ☐   ☐

☐ **Percentage mastered**

Colors (Part 2)   Date tested _____

- ☐ rojo — red
- ☐ verde — green
- ☐ morado — purple
- ☐ café — brown
- ☐ blanco — white
- ☐ azul — blue
- ☐ amarillo — yellow
- ☐ anaranjado — orange
- ☐ negro — black
- ☐ rosado — pink

☐ **Percentage mastered**

Classroom Objects   Date tested _____

- ☐ silla — chair
- ☐ mesa — table
- ☐ tijeras — scissors
- ☐ libro — book
- ☐ lápiz — pencil
- ☐ borrador — eraser

☐ **Percentage mastered**

Family   Date tested _____

- ☐ padre — father
- ☐ chico — boy
- ☐ abuelo — grandpa
- ☐ madre — mother
- ☐ chica — girl
- ☐ abuela — grandma

☐ **Percentage mastered**

Food   Date tested _____

- ☐ queso — cheese
- ☐ leche — milk
- ☐ papa — potato
- ☐ jugo — juice
- ☐ pan — bread
- ☐ pollo — chicken
- ☐ ensalada — salad

☐ **Percentage mastered**

Clothing   Date tested _____

- ☐ camisa — shirt
- ☐ pantalones — pants
- ☐ vestido — dress
- ☐ calcetines — socks
- ☐ zapatos — shoes
- ☐ gorro — cap

☐ **Percentage mastered**

Community   Date tested _____

- ☐ escuela — school
- ☐ museo — museum
- ☐ casa — house
- ☐ tienda — store
- ☐ biblioteca — library
- ☐ parque — park

☐ **Percentage mastered**

Supplemental Books to Use with Lessons

	Title	Author	Language
Introductions And Greetings	*Say Hola to Spanish*	Susan Middleton Elya	bilingual
	Say Hola to Spanish, Otra Vez	Susan Middleton Elya	bilingual
Numbers	*¿Cuántos hay?*	Debbie MacKinnon and Anthea Sieveking	Spanish
	¿Cuántos son?	Maribel Suárez	Spanish
	Cuenta con Gato Galano	Donald Charles	Spanish
	Mis primeros números	Isidro Sánchez and Horacio Elena	Spanish
	Numbers – Los números	Barron's First Bilingual Books	bilingual
	Three Friends – Tres amigos	María Cristina Brusca and Tony Wilson	bilingual
	Uno, dos, tres: One Two Three	Pat Mora	bilingual
Colors	*Colors – Los colores*	Barron's First Bilingual Books	bilingual
	Gato Galano observa los colores	Donald Charles	Spanish
	Los colores	Maribel Suárez	Spanish
	Mis primeros colores	Isidro Sánchez and Horacio Elena	Spanish
	¿Qué color? – What Color?	Alan Benjamin	bilingual
Classroom Objects	*Boomer va a la escuela*	Constance W. McGeorge	Spanish
	Enviarme a ti	Woody Guthrie	Spanish
Family	*Family—La familia*	Barron's First Bilingual Books	bilingual
	In My Family—En mi familia	Carmen Lomas Garza	bilingual
Food	*Gordito, Gordón, Gato Galano*	Donald Charles	Spanish
	Huevos verdes con jamón	Dr. Seuss	Spanish
	Green Eggs with Ham	Dr. Seuss	English
	La semilla de zanahoria	Ruth Krauss	Spanish
	Let's Eat/Vamos a comer	Alan Benjamin	bilingual
	What's for Supper? – ¿Qué hay para cenar?	Mary Risk	bilingual
Clothing	*Clothes – La ropa*	Barron's First Bilingual Books	bilingual
	La ropa	Moira Kemp and Matthew Price	Spanish
	Se venden gorras	Esphyr Slobodkina	Spanish
	Caps for Sale	Esphyr Slobodkina	English
Community	*Caminando*	Rebecca Emberley	bilingual
	El campo	Maria Ruiz, Josep Parramon	Spanish
	La ciudad	Maria Ruiz, Josep Parramon	Spanish
	La montaña	Maria Ruiz, Josep Parramon	Spanish

  IF21047 • Teach Them Spanish! K

General Supplemental Books

Title	Author	Language	Related topics
Azulín visita a México	Virginia Poulet	Spanish	Mexico
Buenas noches, luna / *Goodnight Moon*	Margaret Wise Brown	Spanish / English	house, general
Cinco de Mayo	Dee Leone	English	Cinco de Mayo
Diez deditos / *Ten Little Fingers and Other Play Rhymes and Action Songs from Latin America*	José-Luis Orozco	bilingual	general
El conejo andarín	Margaret Wise Brown	Spanish	animals, family,
El tesoro de Azulín	Virginia Poulet	Spanish	adjectives
Feliz cumpleaños, Maisy	Lucy Cousins	Spanish	birthday
Gracias, The Thanksgiving Turkey	Joy Cowley	bilingual	Thanksgiving
Grandmother's Nursery Rhymes / *Las nanas de abuelita*	Nelly Palacio Jaramillo	bilingual	general
Happy Birthday — ¡Feliz cumpleaños!	Mary Risk	bilingual	birthday
La Nochebuena south of the border	James Rice	bilingual	Christmas
La primera Navidad de Clifford / *Clifford's First Christmas*	Norman Bridwell	Spanish / English	Christmas
Las formas	Maribel Suarez	Spanish	shapes
Margaret and Margarita	Lynn Reiser	bilingual	cultural differences
Mira las formas con Gato Galano	Donald Charles	Spanish	shapes
Perro grande, perro pequeño / *Big Dog, Little Dog*	P. D. Eastman	bilingual	adjectives, general vocabulary
Piñatas and Paper Flowers	Lila Perl	bilingual	holidays (Hispanic)
Somos un arco iris	Nancy María Grande Tabor	bilingual	cultural awareness
Too Many Tamales	Gary Soto and Ed Martinez	English	cultural awareness
Un día feliz	Ruth Krauss	Spanish	animals
Un murmullo es silencioso	Carolyn Lunn	Spanish	adjectives, general vocabulary
Yo soy	Rita Milios	Spanish	self adjectives, general vocabulary

Supplemental Stories for Spanish Classes

Pepe y los globos	Lonnie Dai Zovi	Spanish	colors
Pepe no puede ver	Lonnie Dai Zovi	Spanish	family, adjectives
Pepe y la pintura	Lonnie Dai Zovi	Spanish	colors
Pepe es papá	Lonnie Dai Zovi	Spanish	clothing
Tío Manuel se cambia de casa	Lonnie Dai Zovi	Spanish	house

Sample Questions, Commands, and Statements to Use with Lessons

Directions: Teacher and students should stand up and act out each command. The goal is to use total physical involvement to help children learn. Use every opportunity for students to touch, look, feel, manipulate, or enact the words.

LESSON	QUESTION/STATEMENT	RESPONSE
Introductions and Greetings	*¿Cómo te llamas?* What is your name?	*Me llamo_____.*
	¿Cuántos años tienes? How old are you?	*Tengo _____ años.*
	¿Cómo estás? How are you?	*Estoy _____.* *(bien, mal, así así)*
	Buenos días, (buenas tardes) clase. Good morning, class. (Good afternoon, class.)	*Buenos días, (buenas tardes),* *Sra. _____. (Sr. _____., Señorita_____.)*
Numbers	*Vamos a contar de uno a cinco/diez.* Let's count from one to five/ten.	*uno, dos, tres, etc.*
	Cuéntame hasta cinco/diez. Count to five/ten for me.	*uno, dos, tres, etc.*
	¿Cuántos chicos hay? How many boys are there?	*Hay _____ chicos.*
	¿Cuántas chicas hay? How many girls are there?	*Hay _____ chicas.*
	¿Cuántas personas hay? How many people are there?	*Hay _____ personas.*
Colors	*¿Qué color te gusta?* What color do you like?	*Me gusta_____.*
	¿De qué color es tu _____? What color is your _____?	*Mi camisa es _____.*
Classroom Objects	*Dame un/una_____.* Give me a _____.	*(Student gives the* *teacher what is asked for.)*
	¿Donde está _____? Where is _____?	*(Student gives the* *teacher what is asked for.)*
	Muéstrame _____. Show me _____.	*(Student gives the* *teacher what is asked for.)*
	¿Qué es esto? What is this?	*Esto es _____. or (Es _____.)*
	¿Qué tienes? What do you have?	*Tengo _____.*
Family	*¿Cuántos _____ hay en tu familia?* *(padres, madres, primos, etc.)* How many _____ are there in your family?	*Hay _____ _____ en mi familia.*
	¿Cómo se llama tu _____? (advanced) What is your _____'s name?	*Mi _____ se llama _____.*

continued

IF21047 • Teach Them Spanish! K

Sample Questions, Commands, and Statements to Use with Lessons

LESSON	QUESTION/STATEMENT	RESPONSE
Food	*¿Qué quieres comer?* What do you want to eat?	*Quiero comer _____.*
	¿Qué quieres beber? What do you want to drink?	*Quiero beber _____.*
	¿Qué comes? What are you eating?	*Como _____.*
	¿Qué bebes? What are you drinking?	*Bebo _____.*
	¿De qué color es el/la _____? What color is the _____?	*El/la _____ es _____.*
Clothing	*¿Qué llevas hoy?* What are you wearing today?	*Llevo _____ hoy.*
	¿De qué color es tu _____? What color is your _____?	*Mi _____ es _____.*
Community	*¿De qué color es el/la _____?* What color is the _____?	*El/la _____ es _____.*
	¿Qué es este edificio? What is this building? (show a picture)	*Este edificio es un/una _____.*

Instructions for
Make-Your-Own Bingo

Use the patterns on the next three pages to create mini-bingo games for each unit. First, for each unit, make copies of the mini-bingo card template (page 78) for your students. For number units, simply follow the patterns on pages 76 or 77 to write the numbers within each square. For the colors unit, color each square or glue on a piece of colored construction paper. For other units, photocopy clip art from each lesson. Enlarge or reduce it to fit within the squares of the bingo cards. Use the patterns provided on the next several pages to determine which pictures should go on which squares of the bingo cards.

When you are finished, photocopy the bingo cards and save the originals. Color the copies (if applicable) and laminate the cards. Your work will result in a much-loved game that you can use over and over.

Make-Your-Own Bingo

Top section cards (numbers 1–5):

1 5	2 4	2 1	3 1
2 4	3 5	4 3	4 5

1 3	3 2	2 1	3 2
4 5	5 1	4 3	5 4

3 2	1 4	4 2	2 3
1 5	2 5	3 1	5 4

4 3	1 4	1 3	4 1
2 5	3 2	5 2	5 3

1 3	5 4	4 1	5 1
2 4	1 3	5 2	3 2

Patterns for Creating Mini-Bingo Cards

5 Choices of Items to Use on Cards
(Use with the numbers 1–5 unit.)

20 cards   80 blank squares

Use each item approximately 16 times.

ITEMS TO BE USED ON BINGO CARDS:

1 the numeral 1
2 the numeral 2
3 the numeral 3
4 the numeral 4
5 the numeral 5

Bottom section cards (6 choices):

4 3	2 6	6 1	3 4
5 2	5 1	5 3	2 1

1 4	2 4	3 5	1 2
2 6	6 5	6 1	6 4

4 4	5 1	4 2	5 1
3 5	6 4	5 3	3 6

6 2	6 3	2 6	3 4
4 3	1 4	4 3	5 2

2 5	3 5	5 3	1 6
1 6	1 4	2 4	4 5

Patterns For Creating Mini-Bingo Cards

6 Choices of Items to Use on Cards
(Use with colors, classroom objects, family, clothing, and community units.)

20 cards   80 blank squares

Use each item approximately 13 times.

ITEMS TO BE USED ON BINGO CARDS:

[colors]	[classroom]	[family]	[clothing]	[community]
1 red	1 chair	1 father	1 shirt	1 school
2 blue	2 table	2 mother	2 pants	2 museum
3 green	3 scissors	3 boy	3 dress	3 house
4 yellow	4 book	4 girl	4 socks	4 store
5 orange	5 pencil	5 grandfather	5 shoes	5 library
6 purple	6 eraser	6 grandmother	6 cap	6 park

IF21047 • Teach Them Spanish! K

Make-Your-Own Bingo

Patterns for Creating Mini-Bingo Cards

7 Choices of Items to Use on Cards
(Use with food unit.)

20 cards   80 blank squares

Use each item approximately 12 times.

ITEMS TO BE USED ON BINGO CARDS:
1 cheese
2 milk
3 potato
4 juice
5 bread
6 chicken
7 salad

1	2	4	1	3	4	2	3
3	4	2	3	1	2	4	1

5	1	6	5	7	6	3	7
7	6	7	1	5	4	6	5

1	5	6	1	4	3	2	6
7	2	5	3	1	5	5	1

2	3	4	2	5	4	1	7
6	7	6	7	2	6	4	2

3	6	7	3	6	7	7	5
5	1	2	4	3	2	4	3

Patterns for Creating Mini-Bingo Cards

10 Choices of Items to Use on Cards
(Use with the numbers 1–10 and the colors units.)

20 cards   80 blank squares

Use each item approximately 8 times.

ITEMS TO BE USED ON BINGO CARDS:

[numbers 1–10]	[colors]
1 the numeral 1	1 red
2 the numeral 2	2 blue
3 the numeral 3	3 green
4 the numeral 4	4 orange
5 the numeral 5	5 purple
6 the numeral 6	6 yellow
7 the numeral 7	7 brown
8 the numeral 8	8 black
9 the numeral 9	9 white
10 the numeral 10	10 pink

1	5	4	5	5	2	2	1
2	4	10	7	10	7	8	6

3	9	6	5	8	4	9	1
8	4	2	3	1	2	5	3

7	9	10	2	1	8	4	6
3	10	4	6	5	10	7	2

10	9	4	7	9	3	8	10
8	5	1	6	6	8	9	4

10	7	1	9	6	5	3	7
2	9	4	8	7	3	5	1

Make-Your-Own Bingo

Bingo

Bingo

IF21047 • Teach Them Spanish! K

Introductions and Greetings

¡Hola!

¿Cómo te llamas?

Me llamo...

Attach to page 80.

IF21047 • Teach Them Spanish! K

Numbers

1 uno

2 dos

3 tres

4 cuatro

5 cinco

Attach to page 82.

IF21047 • Teach Them Spanish! K

seis

nueve

siete

diez

ocho

negro

amarillo

azul

blanco

Colors

Attach to page 84.

IF21047 • Teach Them Spanish! K

morado

rosado

café

anaranjado

verde

rojo

IF21047 • Teach Them Spanish! K

Classroom Objects

libro

mesa

borrador

lápiz

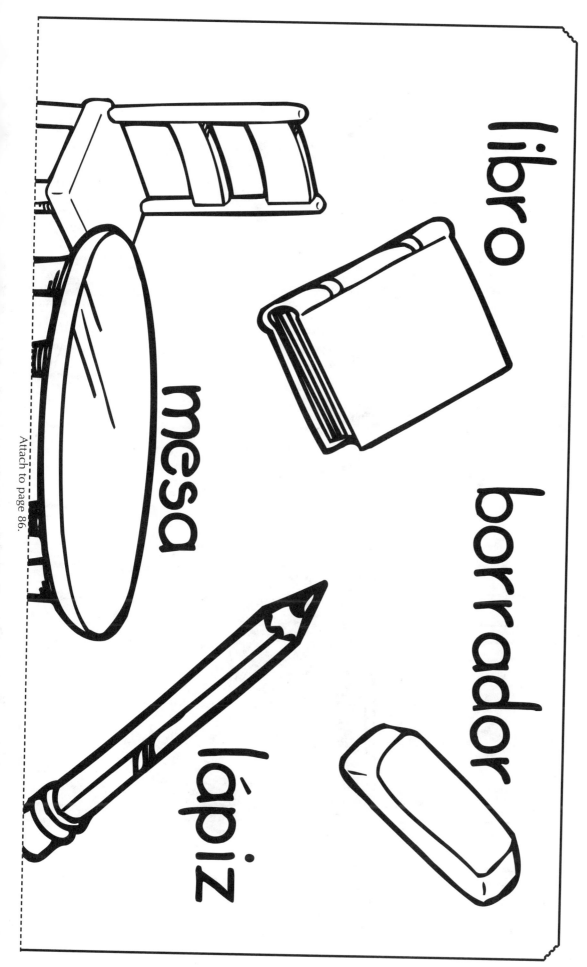

Attach to page 86.

IF21047 • Teach Them Spanish! K

silla

tijeras

The Family

padre

madre

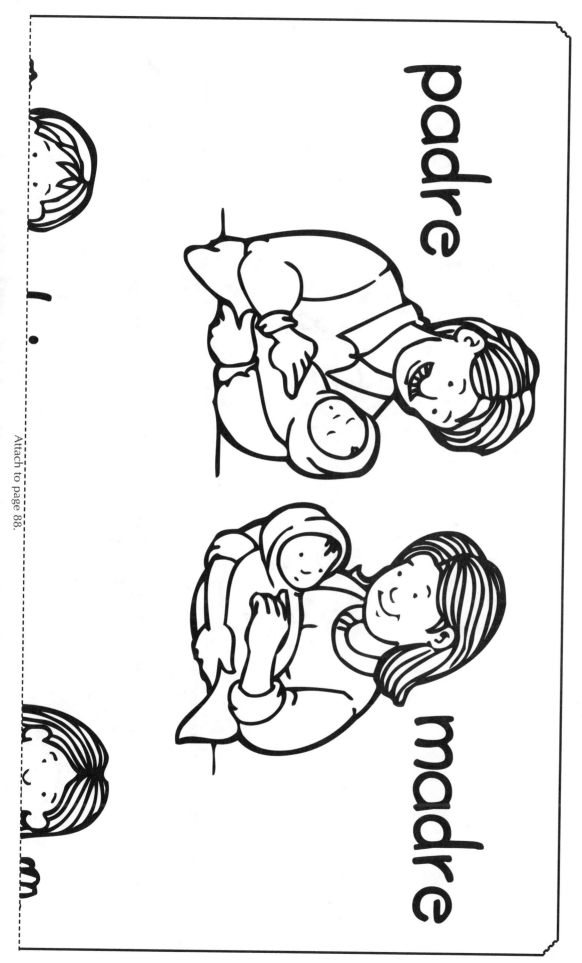

Attach to page 88.

© Carson-Dellosa

87

IF21047 • Teach Them Spanish! K

abuelo

abuela

chico

chica

papa

leche

Food

ensalada

queso

Attach to page 90.

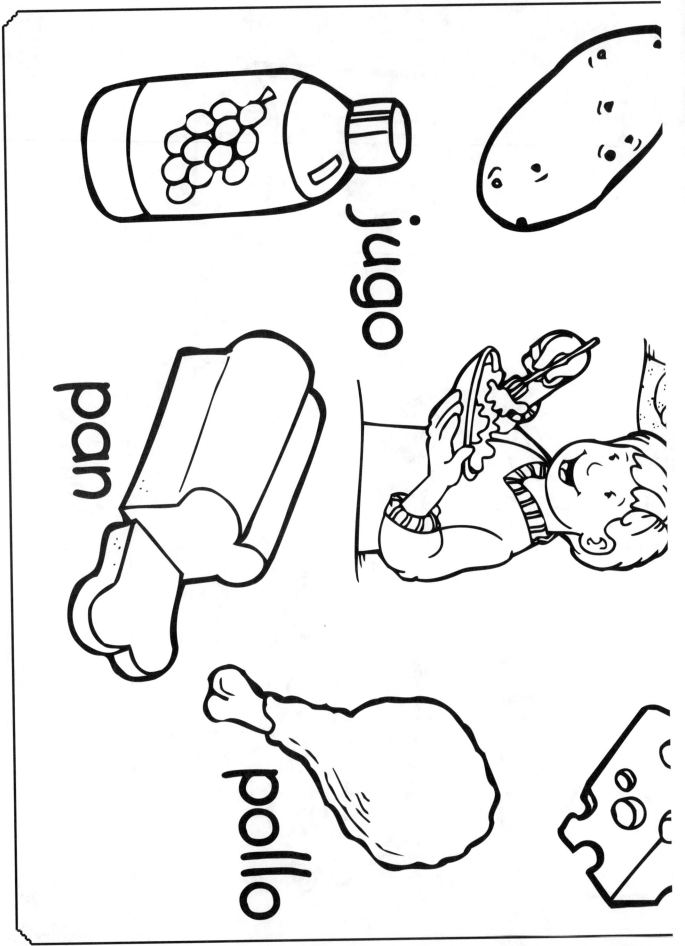

jugo

pan

pollo

Clothing

vestido

gorro

camisa

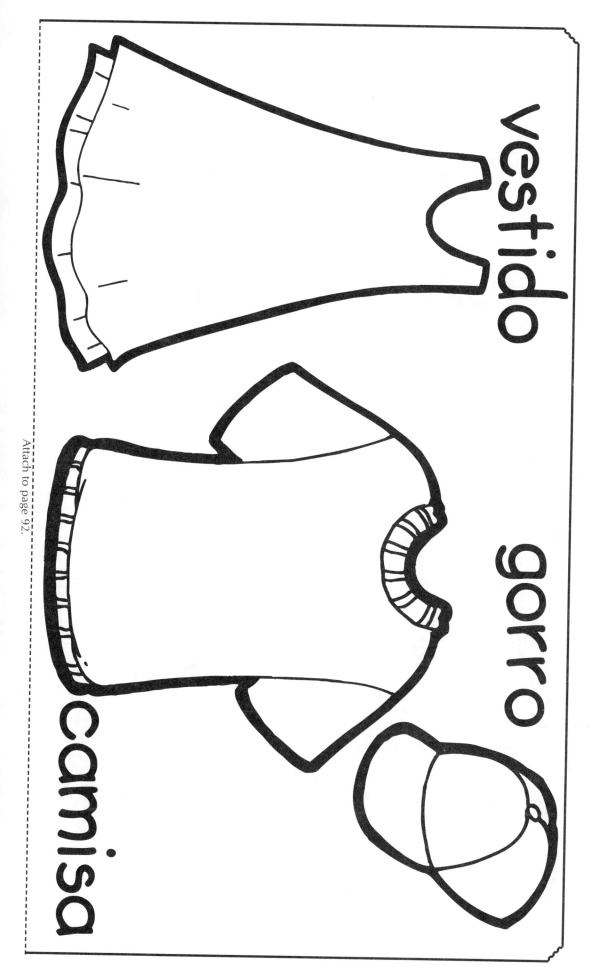

Attach to page 92.

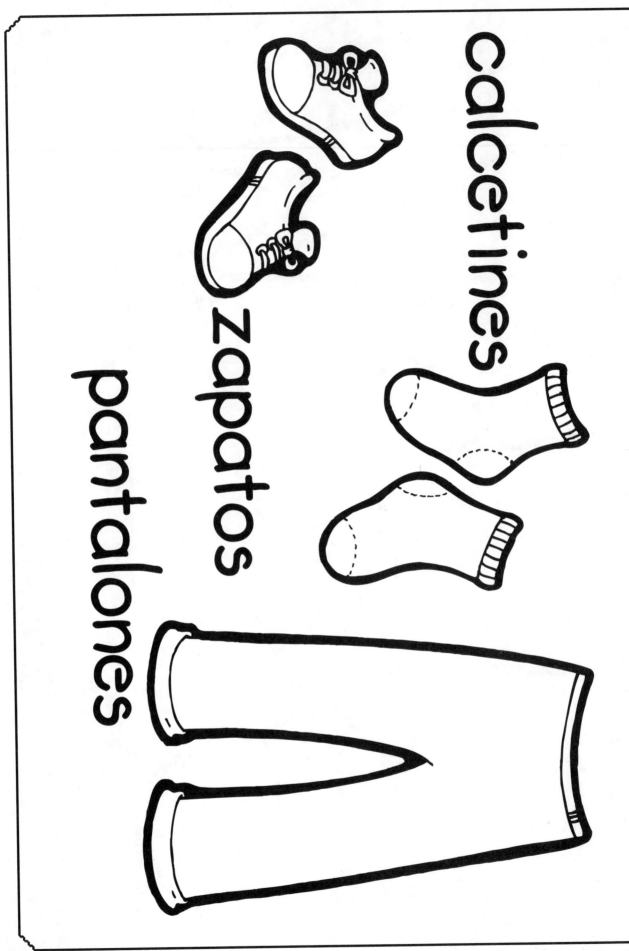

calcetines

zapatos

pantalones

IF21047 • Teach Them Spanish! K

biblioteca

escuela

parque

Attach to page 94.

93

tienda

casa

museo

FOOD-MART

THE DINOSAURS ARE HERE!!

Glossary
Abuela—Zapatos

abuela
grandma

abuelo
grandpa

¡Adiós!
Good-bye

amarillo
yellow

anaranjado
orange

así, así
so-so

azul
blue

bien
good/well

biblioteca
library

blanco
white

borrador
eraser

café
brown

calcetines
socks

camisa
shirt

casa
house

chica
girl

chico
boy

cinco
five

¿Cómo estás?
How are you?

¿Cómo te llamas?
What's your
name?

cuatro
four

diez
ten

dos
two

ensalada
salad

escuela
school

gorro
cap

¡Hola!
Hello

jugo
juice

lápiz
pencil

leche
milk

libro
book

madre
mother

mal
bad

Me llamo
My name is

mesa
table

morado
purple

museo
museum

negro
black

nueve
nine

ocho
eight

padre
father

pan
bread

pantalones
pants

papa
potato

parque
park

pollo
chicken

queso
cheese

rojo
red

rosado
pink

seis
six

siete
seven

silla
chair

tienda
store

tijeras
scissors

tres
three

uno
one

verde
green

vestido
dress

zapatos
shoes

Answer Key

(Answers are not supplied for pages that are self-explanatory.)

WORKSHEETS pages 8, 9
¡Hola! — Hello (friends waving)
¿Cómo te llamas? — What's your name? (child pointing
 to another child)
Me llamo — My name is (child pointing at self)
¿Cómo estás? — How are you? (question mark)
bien — fine (child smiling)
mal — bad (child frowning)
así, así — so-so (child with a straight face)
¡Adiós! — Good-bye (friends waving)

WORKSHEET page 11
uno — 1
cinco — 5
dos — 2
cuatro — 4
tres — 3

WORKSHEET page 12
uno (bus)   tres (locomotives)
dos (trucks)   cuatro (cars)
cinco (scooters)

WORKSHEET page 13
uno (high heel shoe)   tres (snow boots)
dos (cowboy boots)   cuatro (high-top shoes)
cinco (running shoes)

WORKSHEETS pages 15, 16, 17
rojo — red   morado — purple
azul — blue   amarillo — yellow
verde — green   anaranjado — orange

WORKSHEET page 19

5 cinco, 8 ocho, 7 siete, 4 cuatro, 10 diez, 1 uno, 9 nueve, 6
seis, 3 tres

WORKSHEET page 20

uno cow, dos bears, tres cats, cuatro dogs, cinco frogs, seis
hens, siete birds, ocho fish, nueve snails, diez mice

WORKSHEETS pages 22, 23, 24
rojo — red   anaranjado — orange
azul — blue   café — brown
verde — green   negro — black
morado — purple   blanco — white
amarillo — yellow   rosado — pink

WORKSHEET page 25
rojo (strawberries)   anaranjado (orange)
azul (bird)   café (chocolate bar)
verde (pear)   negro (bat)
morado (grapes)   blanco (snowflake)
amarillo (sun)   rosado (pig)

WORKSHEETS pages 27, 28, 29
silla — chair   libro — book
mesa — table   lápiz — pencil
tijeras — scissors   borrador — eraser

WORKSHEETS pages 32, 33
padre — father   madre — mother
chico — boy   chica — girl
abuelo — grandpa   abuela — grandma

The hidden word on page 33 is madre.

WORKSHEETS pages 36, 37
papa — potato   pan — bread
ensalada — salad   leche — milk
queso — cheese   pollo — chicken
jugo — juice

WORKSHEETS pages 39, 41
camisa — shirt   calcetines — socks
pantalones — pants   zapatos — shoes
vestido — dress   gorro — cap

The hidden word on page 41 is gorro.

WORKSHEETS pages 43, 44, 45
casa — house   parque — park
escuela — school   biblioteca — library
tienda — store   museo — museum

The hidden word on page 45 is casa.

The dots connect to make a star on page 46.

IF21047 • Teach Them Spanish! K